MW01235158

Let the Sea Find its Edges

Michael Fitzgerald-Clarke
and friends

DOLMEN HOUSE
Townsville, Australia

Published by Dolmen House Press
dolmenhousepress@gmail.com

Cover Design: Iona Vorster

ISBN: 978-1-291-57279-7

for Nise Seppings

Contents

Preface   **xiii**

Prooemium by Christina Murphy   **xiv**

Acknowledgements   **xxi**

PART ONE

Gaëtane Burkolter	**5**	Let The Sea Find Its Edges
Kerry-Anne Cousins	**7**	Seascape
Glenda Ferguson	**8**	Boundaries
Steven Jacks	**10**	"Let the sea find its edges..."
Joan Payne Kincaid	**11**	A Day Ago
Martha Landman	**12**	A Different Edge
John McDougall	**13**	on any sunday
Glenys McIver	**14**	Let the Sea Find its Edges
Christina Murphy	**15**	the mystic swims to Argentina
Kathleen Romana	**16**	Treasure Box
Thom The World Poet	**17**	Let the Sea Find its Edges
	18	must have
Dennis Thomas	**19**	Cutting through Time
Victoria Walker	**20**	*Anima Mea*
Ric Williams	**21**	& after walking
	23	he stitches & unstitches
Dawn DeAnna Wilson	**24**	An e-mail to my friend on the other side of the world
	26	Dragon Haiku

PART TWO

101 sonnets by Michael Fitzgerald-Clarke

29 Sonnet 88

30 Sonnet 9 (for Ric)

31 Sonnet 36 (for Steve F-M)

32 Sonnet 32 (for Gaëtane)

33 Sonnet 23 (for Ellery)

34 Sonnet 84

35 Sonnet 26 (for Poppy)

36 Sonnet 18 (for Roby)

37 Sonnet 50 (for Emily)

38 Sonnet 59 (for Katerina Anghelaki-Rooke)

39 Sonnet 101 (for Emily C)

40 Sonnet 68

41 Sonnet 27 (for Mary)

42 Grief Sonnet 3

43 Sonnet 5 (for Dianne)

44 Sonnet 54 (for Rachel Louise Jones)

45 Sonnet 8 (for Thom)

46 Sonnet 89 (for Karen B)

47 Sonnet 86 (for Kahlil Gibran)

48 Sonnet 81

49 Sonnet 63

50 Sonnet 48 (for Kym)

51 Sonnet 87

52 Sonnet 14 (for Jennifer)

53 Sonnet 78

54   Grief Sonnet 1

55   Sonnet 35 (for Ola)

56   Sonnet 2

57   Sonnet 65

58   Sonnet 15 (for Rebecca)

59   Sonnet 20

60   Sonnet 41 (for Alexandra)

61   Grief Sonnet 4

62   Sonnet 69

63   Holy Saturday Sonnet

64   Sonnet 74

65   Sonnet 16 (for Christina)

66   Sonnet 99 (for Irina)

67   Sonnet 22 (for Islay Alexander)

68   Sonnet 70 (for Lucy)

69   Sonnet 19 (for Salene)

70   Sonnet 1

71   Sonnet 46 (for Rachael)

72   Sonnet 94

73   Sonnet 44 (for Kerry-Anne)

74   Sonnet 12 (for Kathleen)

75   Sonnet 85

76   Sonnet 34 (for Tracy)

77   Sonnet 100 (for Irina)

78   Sonnet 98 (for Christine)

79   Sonnet 92 (for Dawn)

80   Sonnet 95

81   Sonnet 61

82 Sonnet 4

83 Sonnet 45 (for Jillian)

84 Sonnet 43

85 Sonnet 82

86 Sonnet 42 (for Lorraine Clou)

87 Sonnet 60 (for Paul Eluard)

88 Sonnet 93

89 Sonnet 91

90 Sonnet 62

91 Good Friday Sonnet

92 Sonnet 47 (for Jenni)

93 Sonnet 67

94 Sonnet 31 (for Jane Hirshfield)

95 Sonnet 52 (for The much maligned Person from Porlock)

96 Sonnet 66

97 Sonnet 90

98 Sonnet 38 (for Nelson Mandela)

99 Sonnet 51 (for Glenda)

100 Sonnet 7 (for Dawn)

101 Wimbledon Sonnet

102 Sonnet 11 (for Sarah)

103 Sonnet 79

104 Sonnet 64

105 Sonnet 97

106 Sonnet 17 (for John)

107 Sonnet 75

108 Sonnet 29 (for Andrew)

109 Sonnet 28 (for Glenys)

110 Sonnet 40 (for Ksenia)

111 Sonnet 37 (for Andrea)

112 Sonnet 76

113 Sonnet 39 (for Abraham Lincoln)

114 Sonnet 24 (for The Dalai Lama)

115 Grief Sonnet 2

116 Sonnet 77

117 Sonnet 53

118 Sonnet 25 (for Lionel Messi)

119 Sonnet 49 (for Karen)

120 Sonnet 30 (for Donna)

121 Sonnet 21 (for Rhona)

122 Sonnet 80

123 Sonnet 13 (for Graham)

124 Sonnet 3

125 Sonnet 6 (for Christine)

126 Sonnet 33 (for Olive)

127 Easter Sonnet

128 Sonnet 83

129 Sonnet 10 (for Vicki)

Preface

I am writing this as you are reading these words. There is nothing the world can offer that matters more to me this moment than having your attention. I am alive, and I seek to know you. Time puts on its costume and dances—and my sonnets are both a back row of the audience and bit players in the chorus.

We sing together, you and me, since thought sings, both with words and ineffably. The soundtrack of my life is sung by sinners and demons, saints and angels, and nowadays I listen in my deafness. I am deaf and blind and any prescience in this book is no more, no less, than the next teaspoonful of baby food I am fed.

Sheila Heti, a wiser one than I am, has written, "Friendship is, for many of us, the deepest love we will ever experience." This strikes me as at once hopeful, then hopeless, then hopeful again; until I realise its truth.

There is no randomness of being. The order of the first part of the book is as random as the second part, because before I was born I knew I was to know as a friend every writer featured here.

May you enjoy the works of my friends. Excepting none, they are writers, they are souls, worthy of your attention.

As for my sonnets, I invite you to read them and thereby become acquainted with me too. I am increasingly mute on this Earth, but for now I still speak. Perhaps some of my sonnets might be admitted into your own conversations.

Michael Fitzgerald-Clarke
Townsville, September, 2013

Prooemium

Let the Sea Find its Edges is a volume of poetry that explores the philosophical, metaphorical, and psychological implications and meanings of the sea. The volume is a panoply of poetic styles and voices in a tapestry of intriguing and affective images and themes that bring forth the mythic qualities of the sea and of the poetry that celebrates the sea's complexities and mysteries.

The structure of *Let the Sea Find its Edges* is an equally intriguing tapestry, not only for its far-reaching inclusion of numerous poetic styles from prose poems, to dialogues, to sonnets, to language poetry, and beyond, but also in the way that the book presents its poets and poems. The structure is not a linear exploration of a theme or even of one voice of one poet, which is the usual custom for volumes of poetry. Instead, it is the melding of a number of poets whose voices and visions craft the book and its insights and help shape other poetic blends and departures.

The original core of *Let the Sea Find its Edges* began as the 101 sonnets Michael Fitzgerald-Clarke wrote in exploration of the sonnet form and also of the sea as metaphor. Upon the completion of the sonnets, Fitzgerald-Clarke invited a number of his poet-friends to write poems that also used the sea as a key image. The result is an admixture of poets and approaches, each of which enriches the other poems and viewpoints in the book. Part I presents the poet-friends, and Part II presents Fitzgerald-Clarke's 101 sonnets. It might be said that Part I is an Introduction to Part II, but that would limit its appeal and its range. Part I is actually a continuation of the ideas expressed in Part II, and it is more of an extension of the breadth of poetic visions and styles than it is an introduction. Is it a companion piece? Yes. Is it a symphony that reverberates with the energy and visions that shape Part II? Yes. Is it all of these things and more? Yes. And it is so because the structure of the book is antiphonal and not linear, multi-voiced and not a solo performance. The structure—like the volume itself—is an innovative achievement on multiple levels, each of which the reader can experience, and all of which, coming together, enable a deeper array of visions and effects upon the reader. So, even though Part I and Part II are convenient demarcations, they should not be thought of as true barriers or separations. Instead, Part I and Part II encompass and reveal a chorus of poetic voices, all working together to bring to fruition a metaphoric understanding of the sea and its real and imagined edges.

And what of the sea that titles and defines this collection? Certainly, to early explorers, the sea was a means of travel, and travel is a theme that is evident throughout this volume, together with the personal histories that rise to greet us and to illuminate our experiences as readers. Consider for example, the opening poem of this volume, in which Gaëtane Burkolter writes of her move across the seas from Australia to Italy and says: "I am constantly looking for some way to make landfall in this old, rich and proud culture, my little overtures like the seeking fingers of the sea pushing and cajoling at a rocky shore." Burkolter is not only a traveller, but a poet, with her "little overtures" of poetic expression attempting to push and cajole against the rocky shore of meaning. In a similar vein, Dennis Thomas in "Cutting through Time" writes of "fragments of wisdom" and "old days lost" and concludes: "I dwell in a world of constant inner travel, never predict, sea, change, soul, illuminating mordant, unclosed chronicle past." Like the sea, the soul, too, lives "in a world of constant inner travel" in which change reveals the previously undisclosed conflicts of the past by illuminating the present moments of existence and awareness. And Martha Landman, too, understands such epiphanies when she writes in "A Different Edge:" "I have camped inside myself for too long / shipwrecked along a skeleton coast."

In a number of mythologies, the sea is envisioned as the embodiment of the spirit or the soul that is multi-dimensional and moves mysteriously through the world in ways that are not seen but are understood through their effects. Henry David Thoreau wrote of the currents that silently, deftly moved within Walden Pond, and every mystic appreciates the sense of unseen spiritual movement within the vast and changeable seas. Even within such modern philosophies as psychoanalysis with Sigmund Freud and Carl Jung, the sea is a magnificent metaphor for the subconscious mind—the hidden depths that must be plumbed in order to understand the substructure that sustains the conscious mind of reason and logic. For both Freud and Jung, the subconscious mind is a greater force within the person than is the conscious mind, which is socially created and largely proscriptive rather than creative. In contrast, the subjective, intensely personal subconscious mind, which is the repository of dreams, memories, fantasies, and longings, is the actual and true self or personhood.

One theme drawn from Freud and Jung manifests itself in several of Fitzgerald-Clarke's sonnets, and that is *epanothorsis*, or the figure of self-correction within one's own personal history. In several poems, Fitzgerald-Clarke transforms *epanothorsis* into a mode of verbal repentance that envisions or foreshadows a rebirth of the personality. Consider, for example, these lines from "Sonnet 88" in which the "castle" of the poet's art and life has been built, and it is now "time to leave / catch a train for evening:"

> I see a poet hanging
> from sleep and words,
> perfect words, squirm
> under some celestial microscope
> and if I could live
> I would buy a dream
> long with tremor and risk.

Here is the poet, in the "evening" reflecting upon his life, wishing to live anew once more and to "buy a dream / long with tremor and risk." These are beautiful metaphors, indeed, to convey the idea of *epanothorsis* and the longing to relive and restructure one's life and one's art within the "dream" of the imagination.

Similarly, in "Sonnet 9," Fitzgerald-Clarke writes:

> Before I rise and set,
> says the sun, I wish you all merriment before
> anything inevitable, everything sad. Light. Even
> the glow of a sacred match has reached you,
> so let the silky night burgeon, and while we
> try to count the stars, you effortlessly be,
> knowing life has a name beyond language.

The image of the sun embodies light and also life's passages—a point that Jung made in "The Stages of Life." As Jung says, "The sun falls into contradiction with itself" as light must merge with darkness. In "Sonnet 9", the poet's wish is for "all merriment" before "anything inevitable, everything sad." The poet envisions his friend as retaining the light and exhorts him to "effortlessly be"—which is accompanied by "knowing life has a name beyond language." What can be known beyond language is a type of phenomenological awareness independent of the categories of thought and logical reasoning that language requires. This is the realm of subjective experience the poet must move into. The poet, like the sun, must "effortlessly be"—which also is the essence of artistic expression.

In the opening pages of *Camera Lucida*, philosopher Roland Barthes writes that he "was overcome by an ontological desire" to explore his art and discover what his art was "in itself." Is the sea perhaps an exceptional metaphor for art "in itself" and ontological desire? There is much to suggest in *Let the Sea Find its Edges* that this might be true, especially because all art is without a "fixed meaning" and finds its "meaning" in the readings of each individuals in particular personal and historical times. Consider, for example, "Sonnet 95," which can be interpreted as an exploration of this theme:

> Morning fell other than blue.
> Reality doesn't interest me – I am caught
> other than sky, kitchen table, idea.
> When God became a passenger in a wooden
> aeroplane, all the mothers that talked
> rose and butterfly language held a lottery
> for the last seat, and you, my wingèd
> flower, won. Pilots are happiest when
> the principles of flight are manageably
> tantalising. I learned to fly with God
> in a bathtub, holding my breath until he –
> or was it you? – brought muesli cake and
> perpetual beginnings. Let me begin this
> sonnet soon, some morning, some night.

Central here is the line "Reality doesn't interest me" largely because Reality is too predictable in its mundane requirements and appeals. The poet is "caught" by the ordinariness of "sky, kitchen table, idea." None of these feeds his imagination, so the turn of his mind and of the poem is to the surrealism of familiar objects (God, a passenger, a wooden aeroplane, mothers, talking, a butterfly) placed in unfamiliar or imagined situations—God as a passenger in a wooden aeroplane, mothers talking "rose and butterfly language," and a lottery for the last seat to fly with God. And then the movement into even more surreal images in the last five lines in which the poet learned to fly with God in a bathtub, holding his breath, until someone (God or the poet's beloved) brought him muesli and "perpetual beginnings." And the final line—"Let me begin this / sonnet soon, some morning, some night"—captures an intriguing dimension of the artist's sense of art, because "this sonnet" is complete—but for the "perpetual beginnings" that will always exist as each new reader reads "Sonnet 95." In this regard, the poem follows many of the concepts of the contemporary Language Poets such as Steve

Benson, Rae Armantrout, and Abigail Child in which the reader is as engaged as the poet in the meaning-making of the poem.

Meaning-making finds its foundation in a sense of self and personhood. Interpretation must be grounded in a sense of self however fluid that sense might be—or so philosophers tells us, especially phenomenologist Claude Levi-Strauss in *The Savage Mind*. The mind seeks to make sense of experience and to create a gestalt that provides a sense of order and an interpretive frame. Often, though, it is difficult for the self / mind to maintain that sense of order—much like Wallace Stevens tells us in the poem "The Idea of Order at Key West" that begins with the lines "She sang beyond the genius of the sea. The water never formed to mind or voice" and moves to the line "For she was the maker of the song she sang."

Stevens' poem is one manifestation of a major theme found in *Let the Sea Find its Edges*—the idea that often desire itself is the key to identity formation, and it also functions as a metaphor for artistic creation. In "Sonnet 31," for example, Fitzgerald-Clarke examines the ideas of identity foundation and re-formation in a poem dedicated in homage to poet Jane Hirshfield:

"grow distant and more beautiful with salt"

I halve myself   If I were to write a surreal poem,
Jane Hirshfield the sea.   would Jane Hirshfield water the parted
A skeletal knowing / sea? O how I've ignored you Jane, perhaps
beyond salt, beyond body / philosophy, or its supermarket version,
                                queerly
is sometimes enough. / altered my eyes until their poetries jumped
Shrill—people / into a birth grave enough. Well, how iffy
who do not know each other / is Prague?

                    I take you into my body . . .

and consequently shout / Will the approaching freedom of love
and then know each other less. / enter my yellow, calm action? I am
Are there enough geese, sparrows? / too much a robot to go away.
                                Jane
There is enough of you / you are remote you are book you are
to silently gaze at passers-by / the glass I cannot see through. Your
to watch pollen being gathered. / life waits, large, deep,
                                moon-alluding.

This poem, dedicated to a fellow poet, begins with the line "I halve myself" and introduces the second half of the poem with the line "*I take you into my body*." The shape of the poem, too, duplicates this division and resolution. The poem is halved for the first section, and then it becomes more expansive / inclusive in line length and imagery as it abandons minimalism for the more flowing lines and effects of lyricism. And here Fitzgerald-Clarke, as poet-narrator, explains himself by assessing and embracing the poetic world view of Jane Hirshfield. In the course of this analysis, Fitzgerald-Clarke becomes more deeply aware of himself as a poet even as his efforts to take Hirshfield into his physical body (the body of his work) becomes both arduous and gratifying. In the end, though, Hirshfield remains mysterious: "you are remote you are book you are / the glass I cannot see through." Hirshfield's life and creativity—like Fitzgerald-Clarke's own—remain mysterious with depths left yet to be discovered. And the final line of the poem also captures this idea: "Your life waits large, deep, / moon-alluding."

The edges of the sea are "moon-alluding" as all beautiful art embraces the ideals of beauty and desire the moon represents. The forever present and alluring moon is in sight but unreachable, yet its light and its effects, through the tides as invisible flows of energy, make us aware of the realms of existence—what is near and accessible, and what is far, mysterious, and beyond reach. Within these realms, we seek to know ourselves and the dimensions in space and time that we claim as our own. Returning to Stevens' "The Idea of Order at Key West" we find this meditation on artistic creation and selfhood:

> She was the single artificer of the world
> In which she sang. And when she sang, the sea,
> Whatever self it had, became the self
> That was her song, for she was the maker. Then we,
> As we beheld her striding there alone,
> Knew that there never was a world for her
> Except the one she sang and, singing, made.

It is clear from the poems and poets in *Let the Sea Find its Edges* that the power of the mysterious and emblematic sea is an exceptional image of artistic creativity that is, in turn, "the single artificer of the world" in which each poet sings. Fitzgerald-Clarke expresses this idea beautifully in "Sonnet 100:"

>   And in
>   between putting on shoes and artifices, I
>   somehow whisper from this page the

enormity, the consequence of love. And in
every real and imagined light, I seek
a definition beyond me, I seek
memory, spark, a fire that more than
burns, less than wounds, greater than
the universe, less than this sonnet.

This sonnet speaks of "artifices" and "the consequence of love" as the poet-narrator seeks a sense of self through his life and his art. In the most interesting way, this sonnet echoes the advice that poet Howie Good gives to poets: "Search for words that love one another." "Sonnet 100," like the entire volume of *Let the Sea Find its Edges*, is a wonderful emblem of Good's idea in that there is the full understanding of how art expresses love. In the same way, too, love for the words of self-expression is at the heart of "every real and imagined light." Fitzgerald-Clarke, like Good, understands that poets "seek a definition" beyond themselves that is manifested in their words through the "spark" and "fire" of each poet's soul.

   Michael Fitzgerald-Clarke and friends have created a collection of hybrid poems and lyrical prose that now awaits you, the reader. Opening the pages of *Let the Sea Find its Edges* is to open into the minds and talents of individual poets and of the collaboration they have wrought. This is a magisterial collection, as wondrous and indefinable as the sea itself, and as memorable as the "whispers from this page" that invite you to experience both the magical sea of artistic creation and its equally mysterious edges. Enjoy!

   Christina Murphy

Acknowledgements

The editors of the following publications are gratefully acknowledged.

PART ONE

Abby Sheaffer, *Chicago Literati*: "the mystic swims to Argentina" by
Christina Murphy

PART TWO

Graham Nunn, *Another Lost Shark*: "Sonnet 10," "Sonnet 13"
Moriah LaChapell and Susan Sweetland Garay, *The Blue Hour*: "Sonnet
14," "Sonnet 29," "Sonnet 100"
Russell Streur, *The Camel Saloon*: "Sonnet 50"
Ian Chung, *Eunoia Review*: "Sonnet 4," "Sonnet 32," "Sonnet 60,"
"Sonnet 61," "Sonnet 62," "Sonnet 63," "Sonnet 64," "Sonnet 65,"
"Sonnet 66," "Sonnet 67," "Sonnet 68," "Sonnet 69"
Lisa Shea, *Mused*: "Sonnet 26"
Joshua Meander, *Nomad's Choir*: "Sonnet 24"

Thanks also to Chris Cheah, to Dianne Clou who thought up the title of
this book, and to Irina Nawrocka for being my "barrel girl" responsible
for the order of my sonnets.

All bible quotations are from the New Revised Standard Version.

Confined to sex, we pressed against
The limits of the sea:
I saw there were no oceans left
For scavengers like me.
I made it to the forward deck.
I blessed our remnant fleet –
And then consented to be wrecked,
A Thousand Kisses Deep.

-- Leonard Cohen

PART ONE

Let The Sea Find Its Edges

Have you ever stood on the edge of a cliff? Do you know that sense of vertigo? When I look back at my life, it's the things that made me sway, the times I stood on an edge, that required - forced me, even - to redefine my own edges.

Last year I moved from Australia to Italy.

The sun, the air, the water, the food, the people, the very *'way we do things round here'* are all so different from what I have known for more than three decades. So different from what I imagined, too. I started to wonder not whether I knew this *place*, but whether I knew myself. My edges drew in towards my core, and yet receded far from my ken. I wavered between a bewildering array of states, emotional tides pushing and pulling me up and down and round again.

Excitement and fear.

Happiness and doubt.

Longing and loneliness.

Confidence and embarrassment.

I became once more an incomer, an outsider, a stranger from across the sea.

It's obvious I don't belong here. In Australia I blended in physically but my name stood out ahead of me, never letting me forget my foreign origins. Here in Italy, my name belongs in the European milieu but I am clearly not Italian. Hair too short, dress too sloppy. Skin too pale, figure too broad. Speech too slow, too empty of gesture. The mosquitoes eat me alive. They know I have not spent a lifetime eating the perfect *pomodoro*.

In the English language I swim and dive and roll like a seal cavorting in the depths.

My Italian is halting, *brutto* - a storm wrecked craft bumping along a strange shore, ugly and off course. I am constantly looking for some way to make landfall in this old, rich and proud culture, my little overtures like the seeking fingers of the sea pushing and cajoling at a rocky shore. The Italian-ness of the Italians stands against me like the steepest cliffs of Positano.

I have spent a year already letting my sea find its own edges once more. Another thousand and I may encompass the edges of Italy.

Gaëtane Burkolter

Seascape

See how the sea finds its
Edges along the shore
And smoothing my edges
Slow and serene in dark green depths
Caressing waves
Are like soft hands
Pulling me under into
Eternity?

Kerry-Anne Cousins

Boundaries

Let the sea find its edges – what a wonderfully evocative phrase. It conjures up images of the relentless, rolling waves, with fingers of water and foam crawling up the beach, stretching ever further while the tide comes in, or hopelessly reaching for earlier highs while the tide goes out. Other images of waves crashing against cliffs, knocking down our frail human-built structures in a violent storm and even the frightening spectacle of a tsunami as it flows further and further across the land, destroying everything in its path also come to mind.

So where are the edges of the sea? Just about anywhere the sea decides its edges will be, depending on its mood. I see this as a metaphor for people, our goals and aspirations and our interactions with each other. An edge can be considered a boundary – something that defines a space and time occupied by a person, a mind, a heart. But are these boundaries constant? Are they finite? I would argue that people are like the sea, constantly seeking to find their edges.

Take, for example, the person who decides to expand their knowledge by starting a course of study. In expanding their knowledge, are they not expanding the boundaries of their mind? And who of us hasn't, at some point, tried to change our physical boundaries by losing or gaining weight? Some of us will have no doubt had the experience of travelling on a plane or a bus and felt the encroachment on our personal space of a fellow traveller. Where are our edges then? On a more spiritual level, think about someone who is depressed and their spirit has shrunk in upon itself to encompass no more than a small black hole whose edge is far in the distance, sometimes beyond seeing.

When setting goals for ourselves, we are often trying to change our boundaries, our edges in some form or other. It may be our mind, our body or our spirit but our endeavours aim to move us to something bigger and better than where we are now. What better inspiration than the sea, with its persistence, its relentlessness.

I think that the metaphor of the sea is very good way to govern our interactions with others. As the edges of the sea are constantly changing, so are people, our friends, our acquaintances, our family. The sea can be friendly, warm, inviting, cold, dangerous, forbidding and even fatal, depending on its mood. So perhaps we should approach others as we do the sea – with some expectations based on our past experiences (after all, the sea is always the sea – it is the edges that change) but realising that the boundaries we think of as encompassing others may have changed and we need to keep an open mind and an open heart.

So let us all continue to redefine ourselves and, like the sea, find our own edges in our own time.

Glenda Ferguson

"Let the sea find its edges..."

The sea
Seething mass
Of sea dogs on the masts
Of galleons bold,
Good buccaneers all
Wound round with
Twisted coral
And drowned men's bones,
And every port a lover
For every man.

Ten thousand saw it,
And weeping flung
Weapons and limbs
Into its weedy depths,
As Triton blew, and
Nereids played, and Neptune
Cried out for sacrifice, for the ships
To ride athwart his treacherous realm.

Now its edges sewn
Within a thousand, million
Beavering brains,
Seeking to dispel
Its stain,
Futile; and yet, mayhap
They shall at last,
Its gods already wander
Unbeknownst, lost in poets'
Minds,
Forlorn and beggared, scorned
And insane.

Steven Jacks

A Day Ago

The sky is divided by the trees
It's difficult when you're looking backward
We all have to learn there is no present
The car couldn't make it to the film
And they all were fearful of being alone
While summer seemed only a day ago
I'd like to know what happened to it
Do you recall the Gibbous moon
Which side was the one in the sun
That night, the night Louise's Parakeet
Tried to eat cheese in the mouse's trap
Which ended the only way it could
Well I know there were fireflies and locusts and humidity
And countless guests preparing barbecues
So the place was more like a hotel and children
Were mostly the result of old sex-drives
Racing through the downstairs halls
The last two weeks you knew it was over
When clouds began to look like fat people
In bikinis pretending they were thin
They're all on stationary bicycles
Trying to get lost in meditation
And it's loud loud loud
That you're my tootsey wootsey
On that summer night of the Gibbous moon.

Joan Payne Kincaid

A Different Edge

Thanking heaven for our difficulties and misfortunes is the best way to transform them. You will see your difficulties in a different light, as if you had wrapped them in a film of pure gold.
-- Omraam Mikhaël Aïvanhov

As the sun kisses the desert dry
at the edge of the sea

I find myself walking cold
away from misery

I have camped inside myself for too long
shipwrecked along a skeleton coast

despite my use of daily templates
I find no consensus in the vast desert

so I pay my debt in clarity, my back
turned on all the skies and all the moons

and before long I see above the rolling sea
the water's surface filmed in gold

Merrily I wrap the turning tide around
a rock and tiptoe past the desert sun.

Martha Landman

on any sunday

i hope you receive this in the spirit of its inception - a literary response to the reading of your easter sonnet. this is what it inspired.

composed in response [in free flow - nothing edited] - small bottle of porter in hand... :)

on any sunday:

consensus of existence percolates into the broiling sky
like autumn; skin peels away and is regrown - biology
inscribing in the moment its only truth.

absence, though, effervesces in minds, fizzing the neurons
and escalating the norepinephrine across the sulcii, dendrites and myelin
jumpsuits
and into the glint of happiness leaching
through the skin as jubilation. a quiet mind erupts.

sober recollections dull the evening now, silk sheets in the cavern
of the heart; its thump thump - thump thump
echoing into the unknown like the times she said goodnight...

    John McDougall

Let the Sea Find its Edges

At the edge of life the continents threaten. My neighbour tells me that her husband the runner almost drowned last week. There was a rip, cold and inhospitable. Yet he lives.

My hospital life is between continental plates which are shifting fearfully, hit me with jagged edges, but do not submerge me. There is nothing labelled "joy", but I can see some patterns I call acceptance, fear, relief, terror. They may also be pearls and sea glass.

Organs of the body find their new equilibrium. The nurses call my drug "Gem" and while meditating I see a golden jewel.

I will not see the Mediterranean this year. *Mais ou sont les neiges d'antan* asked Villon: Rossetti translated it as *Where are the snows of yesteryear,* but it doesn't replicate the rhythm and that significant pause before *"d'antan"*. You'll go to the South of France next year, say kind friends, in a "next year in Jerusalem" kind of way. Let Mare Nostrum reclaim me!

I read Michael's sonnets and try to imagine the whole of the ocean, but the word "sea" brings me back to a smaller, more gracious expanse. There are inland seas as well as those of the ocean. They find their own edges, as will I.

Glenys McIver

the mystic swims to Argentina

the mystic swims to Argentina

smile as life preserver

beliefs in tow as prisoners;

in the sun underneath the water

the mystic wonders,

what is there to let go of?

unspeaking the fabrications

found in the silent world

of clouds upon clouds

becoming rocks in twilight

Christina Murphy

Treasure Box

It's dark outside so you strike a match,
what do you really think you have a right to anyway,
on rainy days kites won't fly,
but bikes will ride and splash and slide.
You promised, but what does that really mean?
Stories of romantic dreams,
dark chocolate shared with friends,
and cloudy people rain,
they can't help it they just do,
like black and white nuns,
running from the incoming tide.
Just sit by the fire and watch the busy habits move,
and feathered things fly by.

So many stars, the sky is full of them,
listen to the surf, smell the salty spray,
then hurry up and run.
Time and time ago, soon is gone,
and flash forward, but remember where you are.
Wild flowers in a glass milk bottle on the window sill,
wishes pressed between pages of a book,
cold, cold, November brings howling Arctic wind,
smiling, waving good bye, life can fool you.
What is time, nothing full of minutes,
little treasure boxes, and shiny locks of hair,
trinkets to feed your dreams.

Kathleen Romana

Let the Sea Find its Edges

water sloshes in my belly
wishing release.As soon as free
rushes though earth to sea
Moon calls me.Eye follow tides
to some waved beach.Slap and return
Learn movement and form
Time as a measure of itself alone
Stones later,with this brief life's barometer
eye drink oceans sans salt as soda and as cola
Sugar dissolves.Salt sweats deserts.I am this planet.

Thom The World Poet

must have

time(for breath-slows death
space(for distance assists birth
energy(to activate&stimulate
others(to validate/authenticate/challenge/confront
pasts(to build upon/extend/deny
awareness(fog forget covers all/who fall
intelligence(to seek,to find,to value,to release
empathy(to be within a field of willing consciousness
clarity(to call a spade a rose and dig it!
imagination(to see beyond feelings,to feel within visions
more(for this is never all,could never be so limited nor limiting..
ON!

Thom The World Poet

[18]

Cutting through Time

Crossed, stage, flames burning so bright, subjugation in ideals, moor quivers, water, in breathing tides, stars above, muddle, perfect transit, night cancellation, reborn, in luminous mirror, as tides blow in, vegetation pleasure, odd smell, lust, renewal, nostrils quiver, incense, home, instant smell, night change, recedes, deepens, fragments of wisdom, old days lost, inside slide, rosy beads, dissolving in my hand, fireflies, flooding, in darkness, in a shifting zodiac.

House of endless intrigue, fool delight, bizarre, surreal, definitely unique, study myself, things to be learned, tangent, extremities, honoured margin, wild side, once you travel journey never ends, played out, quaint chambers, mind never brakes, off journey, I dwell in a world of constant inner travel, never predict, sea, change, soul, illuminating mordant, unclosed chronicle past.

New dawn, a place, got little sleep, city of the wise, mind stimulated, past rose, pillaged city, displaced instinct dreaming, I close my eyes, stare into darkness, blackness, stretches, far beyond, my eyes perched, further point, could be, clutches, stars, my mind, dangling in nothingness, I let go, falling, floating, into nothingness.

In dreams lie colours, red, yellows, greens, opening up, every scene, each, every science, yellow spectacle, my darkness, a sign, there is life beyond, deadly scenes, life cries out, as child dissipates, walls of limerick glistered, rain drives, church, mass benediction, no veins, dozing, private droves, mingle, flowers, incense, candles.

A man of insight, seeing directly into my soul, hears great clocks, spooning out moments, metallic strokes, long blades, cutting through time, by the graveside, funeral service, thunderstorm rolled up, droplets of rain, blurred outside world, words spoken from the dead, watch over this child, in her journey beyond, the sea of the universe.

Dennis Thomas

Anima Mea

Take me for a bird in the burning blue
wheeling slowly on upward flight.
Released to catch high winds soft and wild
I am lifted beyond the ink-black night
I rise past stars that fizz and whirl
then on to sweet forever
and find my infinity
in the realm of great silence.

And yet – once, once only, looking back
across the spangled dust of vast galaxies
there is sorrow for the lovely lonely
spinning globe of blue –
a yearning to return to all that I was.

A whisper across time tells me:
Far better to be forever enfolded
in peace and light
while the sea still stalks
the edges of troubled Earth.

Victoria Walker

& after walking

& after walking
walking walking
the sun becomes
a turn of phrase
hello & again
the feet of
a bird are
needed
more
than
wings
a necessity
of clinging of
pushing off into
the next moment
our hard obligation
to ground even
surrender in
a certainty
of having
been &
we have
no "or" to
bend—to break
& the blood
red star
plays
better
on royal blue
& on boulevards
with silk parasols half
opened like floating swans' great
black feet—paean to passion as a long night
& the soul wakes up on a comet
crying to slow down to
go much faster &

you smile not
wanting to
look for
road signs

Ric Williams

he stitches & unstitches

he stitches & unstitches
as if time were
a great coat
beautiful
in its
blue
rip
or
how
he will
come to
the end of
his days & think
maybe i will hem this
to the moon with a needle
of Saturnian joy (exalted in Venus)
the color of alchemical lead
or is it gold—a perfect
beam of her light
exquisite in its
ever widening
arc—always
out & in &
he stiff
with
an old
aching back
& a clownish grin &
at least you have something
to complain about & room enough for holes

Ric Williams

An e-mail to my friend on the other side of the world

I held my breath when she got off the plane,
Flame-haired and jet-lagged from Warsaw
brushing off the Polish winter
For a cuppa in Queensland.

For I know how deeply you love, dear brother,
how powerfully you heart-sleeved poets
Bathe in and breathe in love in crazy gulps
As if it were fresh French fries (that I think you call chips)

I wanted to set your psyche in a locked cabinet,
Where I keep my Hummel figurines from old boyfriends,
Beside my passport and my social security card,
And ticket stubs from Shakespeare's grave.

Instead, I cried relief over your stories of European elegance,
Of fresh salads and bachelor pad makeovers
strangely more relieved for my heart
Than I was for yours...

Her trilling pianoforte made me realize
I was trapped, between my passport
And Hummel figurines; the cynical
Prisoner of Sisyphus

Now you dare me to wear the heart-sleeve
And to fold my Eros into a Dane, a Kurd,
A Brit, a Kiwi, or maybe someone
From a land they have yet to discover,

[24]

a place off the edge of the map
Past the warning that here there be dragons,
And if she throws the bouquet,
I will dance.

Dawn DeAnna Wilson

Dragon Haiku

Pricking my finger
On the map's edge, I am warned:
Here there be dragons.

Dawn DeAnna Wilson

PART TWO

Sonnet 88

Castle built, time to leave
catch a train for evening.
Time to marry the sky
with elusive life – love
pops and bubbles like brewing
~~coffee~~
~~poems~~
intentions – O! crucify me Jesus

I see a poet hanging
from sleep and words,
perfect words, squirm
under some celestial microscope
and if I could live
I would buy a dream
long with tremor and risk.

Sonnet 9

for Ric

Bedazzled by opportunity, by chance, miracles
vivifying in our miracle-strewn world find
you, give you cause. Some of us are lightning
rods attracting more than the sum of our self.
You cruise into secular holiness—not as saint
but as poet, and friend. It is hot and windy here
today; today you are my cool compass, pointing
to the centre of being. Before I rise and set,
says the sun, I wish you all merriment before
anything inevitable, everything sad. Light. Even
the glow of a sacred match has reached you,
so let the silky night burgeon, and while we
try to count the stars, you effortlessly be,
knowing life has a name beyond language.

Sonnet 36

for Steve F-M

> O send out your light and your truth; let them lead me; let them
> bring me to your holy hill and to your dwelling.
>   -- Psalm 43:3

I am your heart, says my poetic licence, and I feel
you would have me honour Jesus, rather than
eulogise you. I wish to say, before a quirky
meditation on the verse in Psalm 43, that some
human beings make simple words, words
that have lost their meaning in this
extreme, fantabulous age, regain their
meaning. You are a good man, a decent man.
To be guided to a holy mountain. I feel
the breath of Joni Mitchell's castle-filled air,
and the life force of the friendship of Tenzing
Norgay and Edmund Hillary. An Everest
sings every day for each of us,
let us gather, let us sing in the light.

Sonnet 32

for Gaëtane

Hope is on a branch higher than I can
reach, said the beautiful woman to
the tree. It will fall to you as my leaves
will, the tree said. So the beautiful,
sensitive woman stood and stood, and
the weather eventually grew cold, and the
tree finally shed. She had learned. Now
she lives far away, and the fountains
flow into her pocket, and the cobblestones
ring for her. And in the morning of the
rest of her life, every tree is beautiful
like her; and though she cannot hear it,
planets beyond our solar system sing of
her, and Rome, and of all those that sigh.

Sonnet 23

for Ellery

The grain of sand the wildflower in
a boy's smile. Are we ever in
heaven when we know little but
take in much? I once was an angel,
now I spend my days trying to reattach
my wings. In the vastness of your tiny
handspan are all the handyman's tools I
need for wing surgery—little man
you are my doctor, my teacher, my first
and second and all and only reason.
When you read the paths before you,
their language often will be foreign—as
you learn, remember to regather peace,
your angel is wide-eyed and wise.

Sonnet 84

for SpeedPoets

I fall clear.
In the thistles, a ghost offers me a coat
I zip a revolution, my life
dug from my bed.
Bread and blood—
the wind in the thistles.

    [volta]

Peace, until oodles of rat meat
threaten acceptance
and knowledge
licks my roof
I put on my coat
catch a bus to a TV show
and fish and cats and fish and cats
breathe tidily don't void autumn

Sonnet 26

for Poppy

When your mistress wishes silk, you blink
perfect eyes, and let her pet you—
the harmony in your movement is
older than your Chinese ancestry, yet
your each breath speaks an immediate,
pure love many could know, but
just one does. A Pisces, I know, with
the essence of my faraway heart,
that you have what I have, and
much more, as I am a mere human,
and you are a Shih Tzu that gently,
lovingly, even excitedly, reciprocates
each sub-atomic essence of love
offered, simple and beyond mystery.

Sonnet 18

for Roby

I listen; and I offer. Sydney is a cornucopia
or a nightmare of chance; your lives are
known to me because your cards were dealt
adversely—as another hand is played, I help
you heal, knowing life will play many more
roiling tricks; for which my gift to you is spiritual
centredness; equanimity. As I walk in the bright,
sultry evenings, I watch the reflections on the harbour,
and drink in its freedom. I have opened many cages;
helped nourish many to wholeness, and they all are
with me now, invisible connected companions.
It is only when my head is upon my pillow that
I merge beyond human connection: I am a boat,
I am many lights shining upon the waters of self.

Sonnet 50

for Emily

Jon the delectable pixie left his clan –
wiggled his delectable butt at the elves too –
left for the highway life. When the
Oldsmobile sideswiped a bison, Jon ran
to the nearest redwood and chopped it
down. A Park Ranger was so enamoured
with Jon's butt she took off her uniform
and ushered him into her light aircraft.
She set the controls for Finland. Wow,
there's plenty of gas in this pixie, she said
besotted by Jon's butt high above the
North Atlantic. Finland was a gas! A tad
cold for naked Danielle, but Jon, ever the
creative one, blew her sunbeams between puffs.

Sonnet 59

for Katerina Anghelaki-Rooke (a homage)

Spiders sleep in my dreams, and I know
spiders never sleep. I dream
of a naked woman in air—
her embrace at erotic centre.
When, when, now, now, my world buzzes
with scent and flesh, the dark hairs
close to her pleasure are burning: a
spindly, silken fire that I breathe in
and never wish to wash away. I
hammer and pound her—I reach her
in juice and tongue I kill her
last wish and then we walk in the
moonlight while we sleep. If I speak, the
me in her will die: let me quietly dream.

Sonnet 101

for Emily C

"leave the world a better place than I found it"

On June 22, Ruth ran away. For where? I asked
myself as I looked at the white vase of pale pink
peonies. OK. Western Australia perhaps? Hong Kong?
Karlstad? The Galapagos Islands? Time to let
my coffee get cold and swap my routine for
a ticket to this beautiful world.

I got

as far as Exmouth. She was there, under
the water – the whale sharks had claimed her.
Yes, Ruth, the sea is home.

The Poet's Last Testament

My perspicacity is a grain of sand
The zeitgeist is lost in the breeze
& my soul is bioluminescent
& my light blue seersucker topcoat still fits me
& . . . & . . . this is high kitsch, give it away

Sonnet 68

Come and have some cold corn and tell us how everything is in the
wine cellar
   -- Susan Trott

She slapped ears of wheat.
An instant dischord.

A Chateau Cos d'Estournel blanc poem is emerging from the adjacent
   beach.
When A Bard, seemingly elusive as that famous Korean kick boxer,
   decided
not to
finish his last

apology — unexpectedly, it must be said —

                    *

Vivienne, the ladybug, had said from day one
her touch, assured as Beethoven's,
would let her, not Any Bard, establish
kick boxing in the Maldives.

So, with a cheery "thankyou,"
Vivienne moved all her tables and chairs
into the nearest ice rink,
and oddly set sail.

—Which brings me to the question.
What is the true dazzling essence of the incognito?

Sonnet 27

for Mary

What islands are unknown? John
Donne's island? Magnetic Island? Australia?
Too many questions, perhaps, but I will
pose another two. How many planets form
from the breath of your name? What time
fires you? In the middle of a sea, you
float because idea is a heaven with many
rooms, consequences. I leap from eternity into
the ground. Mist—is it mist?—falls like
rain. I cannot offer you much until nameless
blood satisfies art. You form from the essence
of Jupiter were it closer to the sun
than Earth. How many bridges cross water?
How many waiting wombs will birth butterflies?

Grief Sonnet 3

My pen is a stinking stick of piss.
My poetry is fucking nothing. All
the circus clowns on all the mountains
are laughing at me. Remember Guns
N' Roses? I have shot myself with
different flowers so many times my bullets
ache. This is ache. In the 1970s,
I was full of green shit. In the 1980s
my shit had turned a sort of purple-
orange and it tasted OK. Now there is
just piss and shit and my pen. I've
left. And the world is a beautiful
garden filled with every imaginable delight
and this is heaven and I can't get in.

Sonnet 5

for Dianne

For this I will extol you, O LORD, among the nations, and sing
praises to your name.
      -- 2 Samuel 22:50

Faux-truth plies its sickly trade often; the winds
that separate us shift, swirl into many curlicues
as the Pacific Ocean's temper changes. And yet,
you are calm with your godchildren, you take
the miracle of each day and transform it into
a greater gift. Now I leave you
for Poetry, knowing my reluctance to rhyme
may dissolve in time, like night dissipating into
my warm heart. My blood sustains me,
Christ's blood gives our world words, and breath.
I am more than halfway through a troubled life,
but each morning I begin again. Faith is merely
everything under and above our wide sky;
and hope, and charity, as my words again fly.

Sonnet 54

for Rachel Louise Jones (a homage)

"Sleeping without dreaming / dreaming
without sleeping / I exactly exist"

I exactly exist. I pick words
up and

*

take them for a walk to the top
of the driveway and

am faced with the choice
between infinity and the wheelie bin.

*

If Shakespeare had met Rachel she would
have told him to call her

Rae, she would have given
him open mic lessons and The Bard would

*

have shat his breeches from stage fright.
"All the world's a stage; & youth, boldness is

golden coinage

Sonnet 8

for Thom

Heal your eyes by gazing at the sky.
Fashion sonnets from clouds and when
clouds have gone accept time will
go, to come back wearing other cloaks.
Digest slowly your weakness, then know
it as dust. And with each heartbeat
listen to wood, to stone. I believe a man
who makes crop circles into living spheres;
I believe him as I know him, above
the conflicts of people he throws confetti
down upon us, marrying us to verities before
time, younger than the next blink of
your eyes. Do you often notice your eyes
blink? Poetry is here, gone, quintessential.

[45]

Sonnet 89

for Karen B

My essence saw.
My past is sprinkled on the ground.
Your wit is the unvarying tide.
Your soul is your invisible home.
And we enter the light of the sun
and taste movement, and repose.

I was molten glass, ready to become a vase.
And flowers bloom without effort
and paintings appear out of thin air
and while other universes are Photoshopped
all I know is the past cost me
when I flew to Alpha Centauri
in a wooden plane—now
I am a piece of undefiled spirit.

Sonnet 86

for Kahlil Gibran

In the unsteady years, I broke
myself on other people – and
truth revolved outside my
head; inside my head was
empty. I had less than an
animal in ways only beasts
understand. It is early June. Your
low voice touches togetherness and
the dark blessings
enter and leave. My
loneliness no longer . . . ah,
how a flock of secrets understand
the necessity of sky. Much unsaid
helps my voice believe this April.

Sonnet 81

Humidity licks me like a dribbling dog
that's just slurped water in the wind.
I am peach; I am pumpkin. I am so
tight corners elude me. In the dark
wash, light eludes me too, strangely.
Everything seems paler in shadow,
except darkness. A wicker basket has
the portent of a lesser known Shakespeare
play, as I get lost in a supermarket.
Feet play with me, never as perfect
as the wish to travel to a library in
Egypt or a comfy chair in the next street.
Join the Army a sign says. I write
another sign, of fourteen lines not one.

Sonnet 63

every poem has a soul in it
        -- Aijo

Seven hearts towards a sky.
Seven outer hearts, and one inner heart.
The break falls. Each soul falls.
The oceans of the planet gain, and lose.
Buried with each soul
the phantasm of god.

As tears well from the gifts,
new bodies rigid with the shock of god.

"I do,"
seems a mental abattoir. Struggling with
an oddly disturbed god. His third wife was temper,
his first wife was sex—and now, eyes somewhere old,
climbing Riker's Hill, clouds enter his throat,
his gut.

Sonnet 48

for Kym

> the depth of the galaxy
> around my ankles
>   -- Chase Fire

As I backstroke into your brown eyes
I have as many options as skies
to your character. I'll choose
three, because the winding road to
heaven is replete with superwomen
in orange super suits. Let this e-hug
be from a poet to a knowing supermum—
you will cheekily wrestle the Aussie
Excalibur from the oh, so ever youthful Lady
of Lake Burley Griffin, and bring it
slimy with blue green algae to the next fund raising
BBQ to flatten the now dubious rissoles with. In your
cosmology, algae contaminated rissoles rate with dubious hair days:
algae are sentient, like men, and both look poxy in high heels.

Sonnet 87

Galleys stink of slaves procreating with their masters,
meanwhile in the bank the puppet show can't hide the leaves
on the carpet. It is autumn across time, and when
an espresso costs more than a death in the family,
it is time to pick up the oars again and
remember Karl Marx is still imprisoned in a tree hut,
and has progressively less leaves to look at. Tunis
is achievable. It is unseasonably hot. A man with
a rope is looking for sheep and suddenly it is
unseasonably cold. Algae procreate in their own
way – their wonderful small acts are worthy
of Goethe's or a submarine commander's attendance.
Every act has an (oft shitty) sacred consequence.
It's time to throw snow at a polar bear and hope.

Sonnet 14

for Jennifer

All streams run to the sea, but the sea is not full
   -- Ecclesiastes 1:7

In the hour when cloud is not white, we take
a chance on hope, or on a thousand million
complications denying the rain. You juggle,
the skittles fly into the air and keep going,
nudging the clouds into whiteness. And a
rainbow forms—you hold out your hands
and let it juggle you into foreign skies, into
diaries God is penning while He opens shut
gates and takes away your leaf—for you are
clothed by the dawn sun, the ocean spray,
the wonder of the love of children. Dip your
toe into the sweet, eternal waters of divine
being, then fling yourself into God's heart.
This you taught me. And that a sea is a sky.

Sonnet 78

West of poetry, the sun hides in the trees
the birds wear blue boots, and everything
is so stuck it keeps murdering itself with
perverse kindness. Back here, the trees
naked pretense . . . oh, in my madness I
imagine rough little things – even God
belongs up a mountain, not in my pocket.
I shine my blue boots. I fall pregnant.
I give birth to twins: an iPad and a
clock. I put my fingers on my Bible
and they burn. Jeremiah, your poetics
stops time, or makes us shop more quickly.
I am about things. I have set up my tent
I offer you earth, madness in all its angles.

Grief Sonnet 1

God—I barely know how. I wish
to be with you—O how I want
out of this Earth. The days are
clods of earth, and it is my grave
that hangs screaming from the bare
branches. I am not me any longer
I am not God (that is my past)
and please, please, please I am
not you. In my self, worms maggots
vie for air with principles, ideals; vie
for increasingly musty air. I
am fifty-four years old next month I
took and gave, gave and took, and
now I am dead and hanging in the tree.

Sonnet 35

for Ola

Girl of the silent clouds,
your essence is song, poem.
My poem reaches your
Belarusian dream. You
sparkle, as much else sparkles.
You dream from a high heart,
your heart, and every sky — and
the thud whir roar of life —
breaks not your thought. If
the richest young man in the world
bought you the sun, you would
return it to him, girl of the clouds —
your own lights, your eyes, are pure
light, balancing in the evening air.

Sonnet 2

Straddled on a gate, between heaven and Earth,
I lost my virginity to an anonymous cunt.
Now decades later I imagine her mother, her father,
and I cannot imagine them. A poem burnt
before the loss has more of me than
that imagining. And on that night
it was as if Beethoven really did fart:
I had left the night sky.
Yet, when we meet on the streets of heaven
our mutual life will be more than this sonnet—
over seven billion sacred acts say so, but
it's the invisible acts, the organic nature
of value that bewilders illusion and hammers
are the beaks of birds pecking at my shell.

Sonnet 65

and i fell into a nice carelessness of small things.

and i lost her.

the next crazy fuck was weirder than the weird inside. fishing to kill
our great white male, murdering banks, taking my soul, giving it
to Jesus, and demanding it back with a bulletproof vest on. oh
how My Lord, psychoanalyse me until all the sailors at Plymouth
and Portsmouth rise up and dream
bandaged, fruity, toy-filled dreams.

*

OK. amusement, or God? about thirty miles east of
Spur ranch is Captain Freddie's Roadhouse. let me
just say about Captain Freddie, he's the Blossom Warrior.

says it all, right? so i asked him. he pressed his
knuckle, hard, into her breastbone, and fifteen
minutes later our laughter was wetting the winding, dusty road.

Sonnet 15

for Rebecca

So the LORD God caused a deep sleep to fall upon the man, and he
slept; then he took one of his ribs and closed up its place with flesh.
    -- Genesis 2:21

I want to walk barefoot in the forest
and the forest walks barefoot in me
each tree an answer to questions I have
that dance the cosmic waltz of being.
For when we ask, beyond our blood
and sinew is the gift of sharing our
blindness – the courage to take a step
when we fear the precipice, the abyss.
My husband and I drive to the ocean,
and as the surf's quiet music balms,
I see three Kings from the East, and
I know again the truth of destination
is journey. The dappled light plays
on my face. I wake. I begin to walk.

Sonnet 20

I will pray for you, and before that I will disclose
something private about myself. Sometimes,
typically in a shopping mall, I will talk briefly to
someone, perhaps over a cash register, perhaps in a
busy food court, and shortly after we part I will silently
ask God if I can meet that person again in heaven.
So this is part of what I wish for you and I too—I wish
it because my love for you is pure, as I don't know
you. I was asked to write this sonnet, so now I lie on
my bed, close my eyes, and meditate love into your being.
Breath. *Love.* Breath. *Love.* Dear God of many strange,
wondrous things, thankyou for each stranger
on our multifarious Earth, help me to understand
they all are beautiful, like Jill.

Sonnet 41

for Alexandra

Bless your sacred tears, Alexandra.
May the overwhelming evenings become days again
may America bring you time
may fate whisper nicely again.
When I felt no hope, Jesus felt me
intensely into life once more. It took
four years, but prayers are slow moving
trains sometimes, each question a station,
and it's only when daughters and miniature Dobermans
board for the truly splendid remaining journey
that laughter returns that each dream
is virginal, is illuminated, is once, twice
weightless . . . do I see you now? The
world is a place of faith and kisses.

Grief Sonnet 4

If I wasn't a naked idiot I'd fly to
Mars and samba under the blue palm
trees and kiss all the walls of the
skyscrapers and bless every leaf of
tea and and and . . . I can't do this.
I can't be with a mathematical equation
called a poem and fight my denial. I am
mad. And as the glass fogs up some
inkling inside me of other people is tapping
on my inner pile of shattered glass. I
avert my gaze from the fogging glass.
My eyes fall into my inner abyss. Perhaps
I should write fantasy or sci-fi or
go fishing.

Sonnet 69

October 17, 2048.

I swim to Venezuela. Bent relationships quiver
from branches. I play *Moon River*
on the mandolin to prise them loose.
The world's at times still irksome chemistry

grounds my humanity, keeps it from ending.
Everywhere, poets travel. On trains, in planes—
they even seek to drink the waters of the Bruges canal.
I prefer my birth canal; — roll over, my love. Your birthmark

is my guarantee: tenfold, twofold, a single fold
on a sheet of paper. The solar system gasps, and runs.
Great Eternity comes to. I meet a girl in Coffs Harbour;
I meet a girl in Atlantis stirring gruel. It doesn't hurt much.

Escape never does. "It's a boy," a Hasupuweteri woman
calls out, while the fever dances problems over our skins.

Holy Saturday Sonnet

He trod for three days
in being and nothingness and being,
and with each step a lifetime
began its holy knowing. There is
no end other than the moment
of the simple, unchanging beginning—
Jesus, while the Jews, the Romans,
the now seven billion sleep, your
innocence sings change, whispers latent
miracle. And as day is night is day,
you hold us, walk hand in hand with
us along the streets of our conscience.
And your love finds belonging in our
void; — you forever are in our falling.

[63]

Sonnet 74

you can't eat a painting
  -- Norman Sasowsky

A tide went out through a red door to join a troupe
of minstrels & players. The minarets are a dream
away; a salt water crocodile moved behind the idling
red car and the exhaust fumes gassed it. All this on an
Easter Monday teeming with text messages
teeming with the plump buttocks of overweight
playwrights. The tide comes in—
it's been ten years away, wetting the ankles
of the girl on the edge. Something more
elusive than flesh: its alias is Ghost, its true
name is Holly, and in the field by the river the
two-year-old girl is orphaned – let this blood
name her life, and the lives of the children she will
bear, who may become minstrels, racing car drivers.

Sonnet 16

for Christina

why do we sink between yes and no
    -- Petru Cârdu

I dream in bolts of pure white satin—the stars
have subsumed black velvet, their milk pours
over us, and we bathe. I dream in feet of pure
white snow—while it falls night will never end.
I am the snowflake that melts when your toast pops up
from your toaster; I ask to be your butter; for the same
goddess created cream and me. I lilt from a need whose
origins are older than the Earth, but I am younger
than the next word of this sonnet. Among my names are
satin, starlight, snow, yet I have no name for the Other Me,
the one that whispers into deep velvet space beyond you.
When God and goddess unite in a pure white waltz,
it will be my hand you hold, and as the music becomes
the sigh of the universe, it will be me who whispers goodbye.

Sonnet 99

for Irina, on St. Valentine's Day 2013

Today, soft toys and heart-shaped balloons.
Australia has not enough roses;
they are being imported from Fiji and Columbia;
and so I sail, inside the petals
of the reddest rose; and while the cynics
sharpen their knives and throw them at
me from the rooftops; I am a romantic,
I am a romantic, and if I wear my
tender loving heart on the sleeve of my
red short sleeved polo shirt, it is because
I believe in St. Valentine's Day, and
I oh, so much more, believe in you.

Let all we the soft-headed and soft-hearted
gather our days and sow them together in love.

Sonnet 22

for Islay Alexander, born September 24, 2009

The winds bring your eyes a vital laughing
sighing terrible and ancient world to discover.
The winds are the breath of the words I pull from the sea.
The winds are September 24 each year and the timelessness
of years. The winds are blue and black and give Barnacle Geese
flight. And when the winds still, poems form.
I give you the heartbeat of an owl. I give
you malt language distilled from the great ruins of tomorrow.
When the sun gives winds balance, ruins repair themselves,
stone by stone. Mine is a line of sea and stone.
Mine is the strong thatch: my cottage.
Mine is the Norse grave slab: mine are the annals of men.
And in Australia your heart.
And in your heart a world grows.

Sonnet 70

for Lucy

Take off your knickers & climb into
the cirrostratus. And when I did pieces
of freedom clung to my naked body. I
lie in the sea now – I am urchin;
velvet & terrible days sigh at each
other as they pass. And when I travel
blue April, the endless ends, the red
flower metaphorically wilts, & the poet,
almost terrible, jogs to the roadhouse,
points at the blue window frame, and
pretends he is Jim Morrison. I am a poet;
I am chaste, spiritual, not like the poet
who gave his knickerbockers to a lorry driver
and left his kerchief for angels to spit on.

Sonnet 19

for Salene

Whenever I have a coffee, I know the truths
of homeland and journey. I have been called
a goddess; but I am just me. What others see
is my second behavioural language: I speak
bliss, bounce, balance; and I have learnt that
a smile travels the world over: fast,
unfailingly. I am blessed to have a husband
that understands, and every pair of young
troubled eyes I see I can teach to samba to
wholeness. Yes, there are times when my
wishes limp along, don't bounce, but I have
a passport—I earned it; I trained for it—to
a fulfilling life. Love and vocation, twin blessings
I have plucked; that are yours also, from my heart.

Sonnet 1

Questioner: Then what am I?
Sri Nisargadatta Maharaj: It is enough to know what you are not.

I seek to hold the wind
    -- Thomas Wyatt

Am I not I am word I am?
Am I pure as a chemical reaction, love?
Has the world hypnotised me
into abjectness, chasing nipples and fame?
Sharply, the light snuffs itself out,
and I am in Japan, drinking at a
garish nightclub—Maharaj walks
in and we are upon a mountain
and nirvana—I wake, and the
sweat in my hair, and the water
of the shower, and the taste
of my vegetable juice are nirvana
and I am incisively dying and history
and you judge my illusion.

Sonnet 46

for Rachael

An ocean of eyes, and a woman must walk.
How can I know her? By her surfaces,
they must reflect some things inside her,
but at times oh I wish I was a pony,
or a Labrador, so I could truly know love.
A woman and the sun, and many, many
men. I almost know what is inside my
head; I almost feel tomorrow; but the
courage to be honest about this moment is
animal: when my flight was grounded my
mother gave birth to me anyway, and now
I see her, I seize her, that woman, and
I know nothing. You have better things to do
than wash my head out, and you do them.

    I never thought I'd say those words
        -- Robert Smith

Sonnet 94

Knowledge is the source of all mystery
-- Heze Shenhui

My hands, a palm tree and a bloodied cross.
Faith is for the night sky, and as you sleep
winter clouds my pulse, and every god that
leads me toward daybreak belongs bound in the endless
abandonment, a coarsening
of soul — I love, and the total of the
world's designs is our touch a thousandfold,
the quietness of birds in flight I create,
and in this mute wriggling world . . .
a bird: O, blessèd closeness! My inhibitions
are thrown into a sky so open it speaks
of the original design, the imagery that
happens to find our love &
shines brightly welding thought.

Sonnet 44

for Kerry-Anne

And I saw what appeared to be a sea of glass mixed with fire
   -- Revelation 15:2

This sonnet reveals nothing. I am a beast
best seen underwater, through glass. I happen
in the All, my guilt, my treason—again,
through glass. How obvious is the ocean?
My friend travels, gives; and I am a sea that
never is swum, whose tide is over forty
years from anything other than love. On
Patmos, a wolfhound vanishes—the beast
in us wears clothes, speaks, and our neighbours
recognise the voice as ours. As soon as nothing
dances from our eyes, do the windows mean
anything? My friend is literary, loves the sea,
and as my salt body catches fire, I see
something I know now is my reflection.

Sonnet 12

for Kathleen

When I think of you, I feel you jazzily drawling your
childhood Boston, and today I wish to talk to you
about solitude: its claim on our intimacies,
the long whiles when we paint new,
ever higher mountains just so we can step
through them; ghost steps: we are nothing if
not more self-consciously to be
the spirit, the thought animating flowers.
Love has ceaseless origins—it quizzes us in unfamiliar
ways, it discovers other heavens – Boston & Austin slant
rhyme themselves into our universe – and as our Earth sleeps and
wakes, wakes and sleeps, we are fragments of our
millennia; and you are a maiden of the archetypal
echo, designing symbols for our womb.

Sonnet 85

for Thom

The sky is securely stuck to Outer Space.
Outer Space is nude inside my cupboard,
many galaxies groan—they want out—but
they are tied in place by my hippy tie collection.
A cow moos. It's what they do.
And stars shine. And only I can see them.
Wow! The Picts lived in huts. Wow!
As far as I know

there are no honey bees in Antarctica
and Kierkegaard knew less than Wittgenstein
and God knows less than both of them
but
nights and days have feelings
and time reaches muscularly into you, me,

---------------fold here, and read the sky from shadow sonnet---------------

You are in my breath, it is your song
that reaches teaches reaches from me.
You walk with the sky bird—
seven birds are left upon this Earth
you are thirty years with me & the
genius in your ageless perspicacity

shines above all absence of flight.

When lines are drawn, you and I know they are
better painted, and better still lived.
I hold the primacy of Art. You hold
the very breath of life—beyond
primacy all is essential, nothing
is a traded commodity,
the only transaction is love.

[75]

Sonnet 34

for Tracy

> We construct our wants
> -- Rebecca Schumejda

What architecture underpins eternity?
It is thought painted
It is the cold North Atlantic
Sitting on a rock writing tears

I offer not transcendence not stasis
The moon might offer
But never the sun —
You are with deep shade

Twenty years ago my life
Fell flung catapulted
Twenty years now
Beatrice purrs, for you

I divest myself—green is not a colour
I kiss kiss kiss the wind as it blesses you

Sonnet 100

for Irina (on your birthday, February 5)

It is me in the quiet hours. Let me
see your soul in the sirens, give me
the last wish I have on Earth. And in
between putting on shoes and artifices, I
somehow whisper from this page the
enormity, the consequence of love. And in
every real and imagined light, I seek
a definition beyond me, I seek
memory, spark, a fire that more than
burns, less than wounds, greater than
the universe, less than this sonnet. Just
less. A lot greater. Perhaps there is a
comma out of place in my intent,
but not in my smile.

Sonnet 98

for Christine

Oh, the ways of joy! Wife and mother, labels
pivot and suffocate often, let's go
to you beyond even name, and we find
replenishment that needs no applause,
soulbeing that teaches as you walk
before and after that being, in front   ·
and behind it, side by side with it, until
you call to your man and two children.

Helen slew Achilles so many times New York happened.
Prophet, how many more sonnets will this book have?
As many as the quiet Earth wishes, you answer from Troy.
Doubt not your wisdom. The sands that hold wild things
will recede. I have chosen loyalty; I have chosen Art,
and there is no choice but for the infinity of your life.

Sonnet 92

for Dawn

Skysoul

butterfly wings meet and separate at your lips

sometimes

the fires of being probe our equanimity

we are friends quietly, yet,
as I once
tried to write,
"vast beyond being."

*

We all try to find
a patch of sky
with enough air
to lighten our being.

Dawn, you are purely part of a superb, intricate design.

Thanks.

Sonnet 95

Morning fell other than blue.
Reality doesn't interest me – I am caught
other than sky, kitchen table, idea.
When God became a passenger in a wooden
aeroplane, all the mothers that talked
rose and butterfly language held a lottery
for the last seat, and you, my wingèd
flower, won. Pilots are happiest when
the principles of flight are manageably
tantalising. I learned to fly with God
in a bathtub, holding my breath until he –
or was it you? – brought muesli cake and
perpetual beginnings. Let me begin this
sonnet soon, some morning, some night.

Sonnet 61

Guard her, refine her beauty, then,
when the beetles scurry away, take
her, again and again. No thing,
no semblance, can box
the Angel, feel her divine pulse.
Or the pulses of the waning men of
depth and wisdom
joy and superstition
magic and e-sword.
Oh! will you send a letter
to the e-hordes?
We need them: Wimbledon white
I need her, and in the un-
finished beauty of a champion of air.

Sonnet 4

Troubles? Let the world spin, win heaven and
return it to the landfill; no end to cut
and swallow before things cease to be. The calmest
sky foreshadows the pains of perpetual birth, and
perpetual frailty, and the other end of beginning
sings in the beyond until pain flies; elsewhere
words wait to form, a science four times
more complicated than an animal's breath, for
two by two they went into the forest and
that forest ever diminishes. I wipe the sky
from the soles of my feet. Into the path of
philosophers and pigs, disingenuously, I throw
pink rose petals. A woman is beside me. Her
centre is the key to my fingerprints, my sky.

Sonnet 45

for Jillian

I took a test in Existentialism. I left all the answers blank and got
100.
     -- Woody Allen

live in the question
     -- Rainer Maria Rilke

Night speaks; a vase shatters. I am elsewhere, but I hear,
and I feel the glass cutting you. Would you joke at blood,
my friend? I am a happy soul, you reply; but—but—but,
the blood-red stain I sense inside your mind so saddens me.
Please, don't be angry. It is me, not the poet. I wish you
to take your immense sensitivity out into the air and fly
it into the waiting sky, I *want* you to laugh; but—but—but
would you ignore a small possum bleeding by the side
of the road? It is your "laughter" that is shattering glass,
and it is those that love you who crave for your tears:
yes, always, give—give—give, but we are here for you to
receive—receive—receive, and thereby leave the echoes,
the cobwebs, and, please, very soon, live—live—live.
Feel. Weave. And night and day will return to your being.

Sonnet 43

O, the darkening blood within the body.
To be political is to recognise the young
Jesus, the world within him
as he hammered the nails his father
Joseph bade him hammer to help.
Or did Jesus even then double
as a fisherman? This, speculative
dilettantish theology. And yet, as I avoid
thoughts of terminal illness, I know
in your wisdom, and your hope, blood
is the sacrament, the miracle that
your best red wine, your thoughtfulness,
enliven. Tall Bishop of the resurrection
you lift us with you, with unnailed joy.

Sonnet 82

My quiet words stop wars, and poetry
post-hallucination is also quiet. Streets
are filling with murmurs, consequence
lives in your eyes. Our winter softly approaches
until it curls up in our beds. Goodness
seems more than prayer, any fixed vision.
I will end with each found thing—whether
life is ancient or I feel reborn. Give
emptiness a foothold and the greenness of
trees becomes a greenness of wind, of air.
Always, dream soft wars. Doubt many lights,
but when rainbows become green, realise it
never rained. In your eyes, brilliance guillotined
into waywardness. I pray light into your being.

Sonnet 42

for Lorraine Clou

Prairie girl, your blue eyes are
a windswept sky of twinkling stars.
From girl, to wife, to mother, you
have lived many kindnesses, and
now you enjoy the quiet joys;
peace, wisdom, and family love.
A long distance telephone romance
fifty years before the internet took you
to Vancouver—remember that warm,
twinkling night when your husband-to-be
shyly showed, as the music played, that
love blankets every prairie wind—and today
angels still watch over Stanley Park, for
each singing soul; and ever, solely, for you.

Sonnet 60

for Paul Eluard (a homage)

Clothe Eros, and in the charged desires
of a planet perpetually imagining itself,
stars peel away, like scar tissue, into darkness.
Nothing happens, then happens again. You, our
sage with murky hands, plucked light—it has
a heat, as indecision does. It is below
the darkness that sleep recaptures burning
orbs: like this sonnet, once frozen in its dream
and contradiction. The First World War
bled many minds, the psyche of Europe—
France—screamed for five years
until, near-dead, it felt renewal of idea.
You were a colour in that rainbow of idea:
always, in life, storm, but
below storm dwells colour.

Sonnet 93

How well do I know you?
Our unclothed bodies are intimate, yes, but
as we see we are forgetting.
No, I saw you first
this Wednesday, when Wiktor Kolankowski's
jazz flowed from your fingers,
and the North Queensland mountains, the
sea momentarily became anonymous in
the swirling, sweeping depths
of your creativity. This is why
I love you, I then knew, and
then is now, a piano is a pen,
and together we are, in the passion
of wordlessness, awakening ourselves.

Sonnet 91

Yet as a fallen leaf bathes in air
I wonder if it has a name,
and my thought falls from
the adjacent tree and I have
my answer. Words such as
"heart," "soul," "goal," can
no longer buy a burger – I use
them to bury more than leaves.
An honest merchant gives me a box,
and *spiritual realism* is worth spreading
but, sadly, I cannot see; I smell
directions—the seas born of
seeds are worth showering in, they
flow through taps forever my love.

Sonnet 62

Smile, measure the
inclination, moreso as
a red voice
swamps that sometimes room in many-fingered inference.

In the century's city time,
in the fields along the
corridors where hares run,
I absolved myself from an Eden dark. And fled. All the love

of all the imperfect
candlelit goodbyes
I entered again.
And on the next day my wings feathered her breasts.

What now, red flower?
Open Melbourne? Open Chartres?

Good Friday Sonnet

for Justin Minto

the sun's light failed
-- Luke 23:45

Clouds gather, and shift, and a pale blue cross
momentarily forms, and two thousand years
breathes into the sadness of souls. When we
killed Jesus, the sky died. Were you there
when you were born? Pure, you had not
wound or scar; — this is the perpetual birth
of Our Lord. And with each death, each muzzy
idea, principle forsaken, the falling from the
problematic sky; before the witness of time
we stand, and the judge is across each splinter
of bloody wood of the cup he offers in pardon.
But before then, the fact. Let the chants of the
mob be our bile – no escape from that – but
the truth is how to defend our cloudlike being.

Sonnet 47

for Jenni

literature is analysis after the event
    -- Doris Lessing

The nipple in the cloud was quickly
blown away – I tell it because you
know clouds are feminine – men have miss-
iles that shoot through them, many have
a soiled Muse, dripping with geo-political
nothings – I tell nothing like an essence, and
the clouds in my mouth are coats and shoes
and my musings on the split banana, the
skinned paw paw clothe me too. To you I
find things – my wayward sanity in the past
might be a recognition of wisdom previewed
of deep architecture below much intuition. Wake
and die – a non sequitur sings, distantly, compellingly
and it is sense to you as I waive idea.

Sonnet 67

I excised April from the calendar, and she bit, she
screamed, and all the clarinets from all over
had Being surgery, and became yachts.

Why is it that we love? The answer orbits as mere as
our Earth, as mere as a couple holding hands as
they stroll down a street.

*

Let us not forget. Insistence moulds this planet.

Just as once, this once, a garland of artificial purple flowers
meant more to me than the stab wounds on my body,
the dead embers in my soul before it regained an

imprint scarring this once, so your love fills my cobwebbed
being, and all the books, their wisdom,
are nothing as I look at your eyes.

[*Why are all words mystic?* Sacred.]

Sonnet 31

for Jane Hirshfield (a homage)

"grow distant and more beautiful with salt"

I halve myself   If I were to write a surreal poem,
Jane Hirshfield the sea.   would Jane Hirshfield water the parted
A skeletal knowing / sea? O how I've ignored you Jane, perhaps
beyond salt, beyond body / philosophy, or its supermarket version,
                                             queerly
is sometimes enough. / altered my eyes until their poetries jumped
Shrill—people / into a birth grave enough. Well, how iffy
who do not know each other / is Prague?

I take you into my body . . .

and consequently shout / Will the approaching freedom of love
and then know each other less. / enter my yellow, calm action? I am
Are there enough geese, sparrows? / too much a robot to go away.
                                             Jane
There is enough of you / you are remote you are book you are
to silently gaze at passers-by / the glass I cannot see through. Your
to watch pollen being gathered. / life waits, large, deep,
                                             moon-alluding.

Sonnet 52

for The much maligned Person from Porlock

For we drug dependent poets—be it Laudanum, Lithium,
Quetiapine, Zuclopenthixol, Temazepam—pedlars, tinkers,
cable TV salespeople can distract from the serious business
of injecting and swallowing, but I don't malign you, Person
from Porlock: as one swallow a summer does not make, so your
knock on Samuel's door did not do other than serve English poesy.

Golly! I must away. There's a knock on
my door. "Who are you sir, and why
haven't you had a bath for nine days?"
"Are you The Householder?" "I am.
Why haven't you brushed your teeth for
three weeks?" "Are you A Poet?"

"No, I haunt houses for a living. Go away."
"Do you want to buy the Stevie Wonder t-shirt I'm wearing?"

[95]

Sonnet 66

Ginger me, cinnamon me, & then let
flavours of tomorrow mastermind
their desire. Until the feebleness
drops more opportunities from the
æther, a plunging neckline will have
to do. And much do it is.

So, ghosts, monkeys, everyone in search
of sleep and consciousness—hope for peace
bleed into fifty years oblivion (I feel
like Neil Young on a bad trip) and then
gas yourself to be reborn an echo . . .

I can hear clearly, twenty
years have passed, and my
bottle, every bottle, glints
spins into the free, living air.

Sonnet 90

God was Dutch and painted.
God was Slovak and played tennis.
The villages became cities, and God left.
Harmful bacteria were there then,
so they must have been of God.
Now, though, the tennis nets have
larger holes, and when people bless
each other at morning teas after church,
God is not there. So you think
I'm an atheist? Nah. He'll be back.
Did Jesus smoke cigarettes? Ganga?
In the evening rush to blame a
Great Flood is a raindrop away. It's
a watery planet Jesus walked.

Sonnet 38

for Nelson Mandela

"Man's goodness is a flame that can be hidden but never
extinguished"

Are you defined by a cell? Or is
your DNA made from your ideals? To
both answer "yes"—twenty-seven years
gave you peace, your soul was forged
into blessèdness; and your timeless ideals
make you more than a nation's father:
you are my Madiba, or, perhaps, my
very wise great-uncle with a smile
as wide as the circumference of
the world. Your blessèd purpose a
bon mot from God—and in thanks
unalloyed, I weigh consequence with life
on invisible scales pure as their music.

Sonnet 51

for Glenda

They say the Sydney Opera House fell
out of the pocket of Ed Kuepper's jeans.
Before that, art: Dame Joan in such
flowering voice that the weeds retreated
to the pocket of a weedy bystander
with bad teeth and a mediocre attitude.
You have attitude. You streak the sails
yellow and brown, and can be seen in
the night sky with the Big Dipper. My mo
fell off when Chris Bailey challenged
the Dalai Lama to a game of quoits and
good humoured as ever Chris ceded
home ground advantage before flying
over Brisbane, over all the leaky venues.

Sonnet 7

for Dawn

Mistakes breathe beyond my pulse,
the horizon is higher today. A bat
passes—I am inside my higher being,
the cobwebs are salutary, but I can
open my Bible and my suite of good
intentions and be with you. I have
keys to some locks, and while light
and darkness feign to change places
too often, still, empty suffering
unites us as no toxicity of movement
can. Words are fun, words can cry,
but it is beyond breath, beyond any
alphabet that God is knowable,
before we make Him our word.

Wimbledon Sonnet

the only things awake now
are the words in my head
-- Guy Traiber

A slow, pearl of a man, whose car
took him to Wimbledon where Murray
and Mandela are jousting for the
Men's Singles crown. "I have it
in the bag," says Murray, "I am
young and fit and you are on life
support. Plus, I'm having a healthy
breakfast every morning." Oh, how
little-known facts can alter the course
of history. Arthur Ashe held
three grapes in his fist in the
rooms before his win. Madiba loves
sultanas. Wow! This epic five-setter
is better than a G.K. Chesterton novel!

Sonnet 11

for Sarah

The goddess Venus presides over Las Vegas;
my lucky number is 1109 – it will change
when you move, and the roulette wheel you
have put in motion comes to rest in the arms
of your belovèd. Last night I won $5,000,
and like Cordelia before Lear, I love you
no less. Run madly, nakedly into the desert
night and let the stars milk-wash you under
the celestial light of the planet you love, and I
will run after you in a polar bear suit and
bring you a choc ice and a polar bear hug
that will melt you, me, the gobsmacked globe
into a figment of the cool, dark imagination
of every dreamer on the tip of claiming joy.

Sonnet 79

Your Earth went a-wandering, lived off a petrol-
stained black silk glove near Saturn, until, full
of dreamy revs, it a-wandered daintily back.
We were hugging chimpanzees, burning peat
to keep warm. Finally, we all shimmied
up a palm tree and in unison croaked, "God,
take us to black heaven!" Oily water slicks the
canals. No doubt I could learn, with my hands on
the oars. A force more powerful than love
impels sticks, kindling, the heat of chimpanzees.
Earth, as they leave you, remember, for
their deaths give air to your dreams, your
favours. You are not known in your places. I cannot
apologise, though I am a skinny-dipping Jesus.

Sonnet 64

it's the breast cancer chemo.

how can i gaze, no matter how
deep, how enormous my eyes? my
throat rushed forwards, backwards, and a Harley
riding nurse offered to send me her
body until her machine compounded.

another birthday, fireworks.
what is cancer but privilege taken away?
it's the stinking old grime of love.
pushing coins from one holy pocket

to the other, and as i flare, burnt, run over
like a cat in storm, all the oceans in the
world propped in the chair, dangling uselessly
— and she screamed, screamed, screamed —

Sonnet 97

I'm close I'm close *I'm close*
to fading gently, high in the air.
To the aquamarine people I love
your ideals, your chairs, your history
of sweaty frivolity. Your homes get
invitations from animals from the world
of rose-coloured clouds — it's harder
here to smell the music of rocks.
Why do the cycles of life end
when you transmogrify yourself into
a slippy peach? I am always with
child, you say, and it's true
you are closer than me to later
and what impels our sacred Earth.

Sonnet 17

for John

The first quarter moon and my bones belong
in the daytime sky. Many histories are in
your gaze, poet, and I look through them,
and call to the music of the other side
of the long highway away. When I met
you, clouds were swirling in your eyes,
and you didn't meet me then—you
gave me your friendship on a road going
the other way. And we share things:
writing, football amongst them; but it is
my heart, that I gave and lost, that I
wish you to see—here it is, by the roadside,
bleeding, barely moving, barely alive:
please find words for it, please let it speak.

Sonnet 75

Throw yourself at the sky
and if you rise and rise
past its blueness to the black
beyond, you will have proved
the spots and stains on your psyche
are stardust, and you belong
elsewhere. And if those below
begin to rise too, who needs air?
Have a stellar party, procreate &
create wondrously. I hear the night;
and I see the morning—I hear the
fight; and I grasp the dawning. I'm
alright, and long may things sleep.

Endlessly, a sky dreams.

Sonnet 29

for Andrew

After hallucinating on a bowl of Tibetan
Cornflakes, I remember the mushroom daze,
when telephones rang without being rung,
ladders dropped me into an exalted sky,
and the reward for whatever it was
was a pork roast, minus the dancing broccoli.
Upsidedown in my bed, I realise I'm stood
in a queue for new tonsils and seven
rolls of toilet paper. Oh! Shit! I need
twenty-nine rolls to decorate this Palace,
before I invite the old gang to a dahlia
tasting. I've toked flowers, but my bad
carnation trip now makes me stick to pine cones.
Salaam number 29. This is the other universe.

Sonnet 28

for Glenys

Following the Book of Mormon, John Keats
also travelled to America, or so this Book
of Michael's says. Life is one long literary
holiday for some, but not you: roaming
in Rome, yes, but tempered by a dedication
to words, not poesy, that many New England
poets might yet admire. Keats, Frost: among
their bricks and mortar the sanitised
stories that history purrs as it rubs
against our legs, our wounded yet receptive
psyches. We all are soldiers, our war medals
might be in the warehouse of the æther, but
as we learn to better love, you are a teacher,
and steeped in meaning, the ways of sonnets.

Sonnet 40

for Ksenia

The Polish winters crawl into your bones;
inside, you dream slim dreams, secure,
warm dreams, and the snow and ice and
the skies touching your dear head will melt
into pink and white blossom. Some day,
years from now, when absences eat less of the
home-cooked cakes, when those elusive coins and
notes fly less quickly around you, the pure things,
love with all its many, wondrous, terrible,
difficult, essential ways, will be yours.
For now, let life flower around you,
and the way the sky looks at you says
things are better than you now believe
things are fragments of dreams becoming whole.

Sonnet 37

for Andrea

If your sense of perspective were a painting,
it would be a Titian, not a Picasso. You are
a classical twenty-first century woman, and
one May I'll take you for breakfast at
Tiffany's, for your kindnesses to me.
Over twenty-seven years this year (hey,
Jim Morrison's lifetime – you are The
Lizard King, Jim, you can do anything),
Ups have been Ups, and Downs have been
Downs balanced on a tightrope at times,
but I've known I can phone you for a
catch up, and when the phone leaves my
ear, I feel complete for a poised red-
headed moment in my untidy life.

Sonnet 76

A pet-lamb in a sentimental farce!
-- John Keats

Not a shred of poetry is in me, until I remember
the brutal shards on our TVs of Syria, Gaza,
the African conflicts; and then, knowing better
souls than me fire words in response, I know
I must – at least for today – ditch Art with all its poses,
and become a warrior for humanity. It's uncomfortable,
this new stance – God I crave the sanctity of religion
and Art – what can I do? What difference can I make?
Am I playing Hamlet in an empty theatre while a Syrian
kid grieves her raped, dead mother? There are four
lines left in this sonnet for me to matter to someone.
I raise my finger and chide myself, the mirror shatters,
and I'm not in the Congo, not anywhere other than on my
sofa with washing to hang out, and, somehow,

a self to be true to.

Sonnet 39

for Abraham Lincoln

This is sonnet as theatre
I have no heart I have no body
The day after Good Friday stank with your loss

Yes, the details of your life are props for your ideals
I want to be that last drop of rain
You felt on your skin

I want to be the last breath of wind
You breathed in and took the goodness of the sky
You breathed in and John Wilkes Booth became a slave

The crowds still war amongst themselves
You pat me on the shoulder
Your shoulders bear the bridge of time
Your face was facing eternity

Bless us Abe, give us peace, one day we might hold onto it

Sonnet 24

for Tenzin Gyatso, the Fourteenth Dalai Lama

I name each cloud I see, and bless
all the clouds yet to coalesce, and all
the clouds I have not seen, and will never see.
In the high cold, blood is precious, and
my dream says smile at difference, do not
knot a length of rope, do not keep score.
Sweet life, you have given me a people. I
happen in the same way as those leading China—
we are the same chimera here, the same cloud;
and when storms come, intrinsic is their passing.
We will fall from this time. The mountains sense
their impermanence better than we do ours, often.
Be as ancient as your self before fear.
And time will kiss and balance you.

Grief Sonnet 2

Language is mute. My love is forcèdly
mute. Were I to say "fuck" ten thousand
times I still would be ten thousand times
mute. Can you see me? I am so invisible
my teeth chatter in the wind. It's raining.
What's rain? In the late afternoon there
is no life. No life. No life. Why can't
I speak? Am I in a room mangled with
otherness? Why are all my questions full
of naked nothingness? I can't call your name.
I can't bring anything but a soul being
submerged in the ocean of night. At least
I know darkness. It veers into my psyche
and somehow saves me from more death.

Sonnet 77

I do hell to myself—it is heaven
that is some figment of the Bible
when my eyes go and be questionably
born. They return. I return to vegetable
soup: Chinese cabbage, broccoli, tomatoes,
onions, and the mandatory folk music herbs.
Yesterday, thought. The devil has a cabbage
skewered on his pitchfork, and my ass
has been colander-punctured so often I haven't
the time when loss flames everything that
is worth more than tiny summer flowers.
The recipe for life again steps away from me.
Love seems less than sense. Time for
champagne, a toast to hurt, to indecision.

Sonnet 53

The space between two people is as close
as orgasm, as distant as God. This necessary
duality, this black & white photo of being,
means butterflies are ugly, toads are sweet
to everyone. There are no exceptions.
So kiss a frog and die from your humanity, kiss
a toad, and, just perhaps, immolate your world-weariness.
I am your reward says God, yet in the blue-crimson
past I heard that countless times and now the message
is torn, and tired. Let the sea find its edges,
they are not ours says the man. I am
my own edge; I form crevices in things and eventually
heal them. The sun has turned green she says, and I
believe her. She comes, she knows her gods.

Sonnet 25

for Lionel Messi

The blue skies of hell; the thunder clouds of heaven!?
I try to enter your mind through your feet.
What is it like to be the world's best?
Do you kick the soap around in the shower?
I went on a cruise with the world's best poet,
and she kicked the soap; her poetry was wordless,
like yours; she touched me lovingly, and I touched
her back, picked up the pink soap. When you were a
boy, did you kick the sky? Now you sweat diamonds,
pearls, all the music of the box. I am tempted
to leave you for the poet, but before I rejoin
her perpetually showering form, I want
you to know you are me, I am you, and we are her.
Such is the beauty of the game of the world.

Sonnet 49

for Karen

In the next life, I want a butt like Yolko Oh No,
in the next life, I want an even bigger celery
stick to more-than-faux-tickle the smallest
spider. In the next life I want gluten free
steak, sausages, bread, biscuits, milk—
I'm a dreamy girl when dreams joyfully
open possibility. When a leaf falls from
a tree in Canberra, my Queensland smile
rises to the warmer stars. Or so a bird
told me—it flew into my life as lastingly
as my love for my kids. Celery and gluten
matter in some strange, circumlocutory
way, like twilight with its kernel of dawn, like
friendship, a perpetual photograph of trust.

Sonnet 30

for Donna

Same but different. I offer an art of life
painted on the walls, the skies of my wondrous ones,
the spaces of my meditation and yoga. I seek to
define other than this digital age—each painting
is a verity I see when waters still.
This is me: somehow holding stillness.
I give to idea my backpack, and a question is
an axiom of myself with a hand in the lake holding
a sword—myth teaches a purer geography.
A self running to sense. A mother hauling anchors
quietly until the sky snaps open and cloud-boats
are the purest thoughts. I tell myself this in the corridors,
when fleeting—oh, perhaps even ever present—
aloneness wishes to dance in that careful, fragile stillness.

Sonnet 21

for Rhona

> On the water walking, it's easy to be
> -- Nik Turner

Deep within an ocean, I merge into a fabric
few know. I have dived from my youth into
an adulthood of fulfilment and loss—I
had a husband and our story is an
ancient one—but the serpent that was in my
garden cannot deny me the joys from being
a mother and grandmother. A sea turtle swims
by. Its shell beckons me, and I am tempted.
Perhaps you might say I should be a mermaid,
but I have many directions, and though this
water is unanchored solitude, it is, if I'm
honest, too seductive for thought. Creation is
upon us from the depths to the high miles, and
it offers more than diving, and flight.

Sonnet 80

White and pink striped moments are confetti, rice
thrown at a wedding of the gods. The label
I give love dances as it fluctuates in
your eyes. Paint leaves the wall and
settles back in the tin. A boffin has
a bright idea to bring back horses and
buggies. Rain hurts my eyes. My
stomach tells me it's time to visit the
space station and have some gravity-free
downtime. Where? In the cupboard, you
silly man, next to the badminton racquet
and the painting of Queen Victoria. Put
it on the wall. Some things are best
left in cupboards, being mindful of entropy.

Sonnet 13

for Graham

If the only prayer you ever say is "thank you", it will suffice.
-- Meister Eckhart

Heron and poet claim the river, the subtle
celebrations of other birds score the moment
between timelessness and image. As life
eddies yet flows, the quietness of calling
moves, impels greater flight. I bring my faith
in the heron's being, I ply my lines knowing
the Brisbane streets are another article, and
the congruence between brown water and
grey concrete is more than vaulting birdsong.
As heron and poet thank each other the sun
leaves us for our nightly darkness. I pack my
few possessions into a poem and drive away.
Tomorrow will fire, will animate our asking world,
and I will ask, and my growing boy will answer.

Sonnet 3

So he cometh and goeth.
-- Hugh Latimer, Bishop of Worcester

I am in the way of Dante Alighieri, Beatrice and God.
My moment on the staircase is higher than them
all and it is this—the plunge into the world—that seals
my fate. Some butterfly pinned on a tray in a
museum cabinet knew life, and as I teach myself
from the bottom of an abyss to accept time and space
and how love makes the bottom of an abyss as shallow
as a bathtub, as fathomless as invisible angels,
I talk to my angel not as Dante but as
a mender of a broken window, and through
the open window the sounds of the world—Bach,
Handel, Eminem, Flo Rida, Jesus—all are there beyond
the rasp of lorries, the thoughts of butterflies.
The non sequitur of silence touches a sonnet into being.

Sonnet 6

for Christine

What is illusion? Is it buried within the happiness
we share in moments when cold numbs our fingers
when memories make our tears sweet? Yesterday
I swallowed broken glass, wet my bed, and
auditioned for *Pope Soap On A Rope The Musical.*
I flew to Serbia with a cute Jehovah's Witness, then
to England where I wrestled a cucumber sandwich
from the Queen, breaking her wrist. Such are
the broken yesterdays away from time—it is time
that gives the definiteness we seek air, and earth,
and water. And as we breathe, as we watch our
breath, all is calm—hug your two sons, Christine,
follow the timeless footsteps of love, elusive yet
charmingly divine. All else is without design.

Sonnet 33

for Olive

> Early, before the sky
> -- Graham Nunn

I am passive with a pen
I know nothing in this room but the air con
Your trust, respect makes me know less
Your words give; I become supple

On a Wednesday evening, I shift
In a chair I dance afflatus
Over a black coffee sugar grains
And when I crawl back in my pram —

Prams aren't real my sonnet
Makes them up before a sky
Before your poems make me so real
I am a critic

And I forget—nothing like being forgotten
Says the poem to the poet's auburn narrative

Forget me, stay, with your past a gecko's promises are words

Easter Sonnet

I see your resurrection in a newborn baby's smile
I see your resurrection in the strawberry-fresh contentment
of a mother's joy, I see it in the early morning sky
that cleanses thought and deed. I see
your resurrection in the fish biting in a mountain stream,
in the poetry of a fisherman's cast. I see your resurrection
in an e-mail from a belovèd friend, the gifts of her
time and her thoughtfulness. And as I see all of this,
your resurrection enters my empty heart and finds
a hope in my little world of poems. And
your resurrection balms my later years and I feel
the weight of a cross become a living, budding tree
that blossoms then gives dark, shiny, juicy plums. I see
your resurrection Jesus, and I name it, claim it, give it,
and my little world rejoices as the big planet sings.

Sonnet 83

I am endless – my life in snow
my life in fire, I know chasm
I know cloud, I know surpassing dreams.
It is knowing midnight is white
it is being nourished by words
unafraid of jumping into moments
burnished by infinity. My brothers,
my sisters, be invisible, be escapees
expansively, with care. Freedom
is a second heart, as is death.
I am ending by whispering silently
my intimations above the sky
I drink emptiness, and, happy,
rain and light open in being.

Sonnet 10

for Vicki

I have many shadows; I face only a few.
I am poemscaping my life, and, today, yours—
you meld into me, your love of books, music,
and art is my love, your sensitivity is mine;
but it is when we dream precognitively
we are most akin. Three times,
I dreamt it was my birthday.
Three next days, I got news my poetry
collections were to be published. Let us be
romantics, let us laugh at as many shadows
as try to possess us. You care for our
planet, and in the thought-fabrics you weave
our humanity is inexhaustible, and the
greatness of shadow no longer is grey.

Made in the USA
Columbia, SC
02 June 2025